Imitations of Love Poems

Dory Williams and Dustin Pickering

TRANSCENDENT ZERO PRESS

HOUSTON, TEXAS

ISBN-13: 978-1-946460-08-0
Library of Congress Control Number: 2018913353

Printed in the United States of America

Transcendent Zero Press
16429 El Camino Real Apt. #7
Houston, TX 77062

FIRST EDITION

Imitations of Love Poems

Dory Williams and Dustin Pickering

Contents

The Smile

What's in the mind behind a smile?
If a stranger sees me sad, maybe a smile
is a person's past crying. Or simply the charity
of God trying. But I know that beneath a smile
there is my Life underlying.
When I know I give a smile, I need no help.
But if they can finally help me,
                    they come running,
to my sadness that I hide by clever cunning.
And I know what's underlying!
Because not all Life is on the surface.
A smile is deeper, like our purpose.

        And when I exit this Life,
        (and it should take a while)
maybe I won't be cowardly if I see a smile.
No! I'll be grand when you give me your hand
to my good-bying. And like a smile, there
is always Life underlying.

The Royal Covers

I was singing underwater with only Hope.
A king dragged me out and wrote down all my stupidity
on a moat. Then he stole the brightest light from the sun,
dimmed it, then reflected it on a piece of wood.
Magic Light says by my eyes, "This time a man understood!"
That made it through to my wooden head, and with my
anxious ears, he said my bed (As his command).
He covered my head with royal blankets beneath
words of Love. He cured me with sure hands,
fit a purposeful glove. Then he healed scars
from those people who were mean.
I was his girl but Love was his routine.
So if his Love was True, for once something did not have
its price (before we get old and sacrifice).
And if his Love was fake, my mind's been gone,
crushed down the royal covers like a snake.

The Power of Acting

Your parents and you decided for you
to spread Love in the world and,
when you were young, you made a pact.
But that boy said he Loved you and it was all an act!
After heartache from that boy, they said that,
not thinking of him anymore, you'd like it.
Look in the mirror and say, "Everything will be O.K."!
Now act like it!!

Love at First Sight

We have these deep, inner thoughts
that prove our characters.
But maybe I can sum that up in one glance!
Because it is a look you give
(not your deep, inner thought)
that makes my heart dance.
So, if I can
trust what I can see
then I can take a chance.

What is shallow
in you can be made
to be skin deep. Maybe I can fill in
the spaces. It's what's on the surface
of you that I see when my own heart races.
Besides, maybe we wear our characters
on our faces! All this time and effort
                    to better ourselves
                    and the world . . . .
But really, what isn't initial?
You put spirit in my look.
So, maybe
    Love is supposed to be superficial!

Dies by the Sword

There is justice in "an eye for an eye"
if that is Nature's rule and She gives us her word.
But there is more justice in never picking up that sword!

Mad Fate

After my passion for you has abated,
And I don't remember all those years
I waited,
And I don't remember all those mistakes
I've dated.
Only what I've loved, what I've hated . . . .

So, my life, it may not be celebrated,
And I'm sure my death will be very tolerated!

My question is . . . .
When the light inside burns out . . . .
Was that deliberated or fated?

Things are Hard

You just start out following your dream
and you say that it is hard in every way.
Well, isn't Life hard anyway??
That man rejected me. So I guess,
for my own amusement, I was wooing.
Still, if things are hard everywhere,
I'd rather be doing what I want to be doing!
For some people, things come easy.
They find out Life is hard and it's news to them.
And for others, things are hard, but they get used to them.
These people, they need us (because sometimes)
the Good things,
I think God must have to force-feed us!

Looks Aren't Knowledge

A rejection is supposedly negative.
But sometimes it's positive.
Wouldn't it be great
if we didn't Love
someone
for their looks, but for their virtue?

For me to know the Truth
about you is long overdue.
And why you don't like me,
I haven't got a clue!

Maybe, when you rejected me,
   you protected me
    from you!
You see, I don't know you.
And, if I did, I might not know
what's worse.
If I could say this dream came True,
would that be a blessing or a curse?

The Border of the Neck
inspired by the movie The Devil's Advocate

There is a border at your neck
where my lips dare to travel, Where begins a mystery
you hesitate to unravel. But only if I cross the world's line
in the sand, The one that muffled my heart gone south.
I looked forward to a night on the beach,
Ruled by a band, And kisses so near to the bravery
of your mouth, Where I confess the sad reality
of each fear . . . . If I could just speak,
In a prayer to the tolerance of your ear,
That made me so strong, I got weak.

Church Perspective

When I am too desperate to receive salvation,
        they are there to be desperate.
When I doubt our faith, they are there with faith.
When I want to curse my Creator, they are there
        To remind me I have blessings.
When I fear my atonement, they earn it with me.
When a sermon exposes torment, they share!

But when I couldn't secure you as my boyfriend,
they laughed. And that pain made me into a preacher!

Judge

If you were a judge
sentencing someone
To death, why would you say,
"May God have mercy on your soul"
                    if you didn't?

My Path

While I'm on my path, old friends may cross
My path frequently, then, not at all.
Then my path crossed your path, and you altered it
Effortlessly. Until I just wanted to be on God's path,
Which encompasses everyone's path.
                    Me and we,
                    You and her,
            Them and she, and he and I struggle
To see the road until we converge, and say our thanks
To Him without any strings attached.

What comes first is tolerance

Sometimes
what is
suppose
to bring
us together
is what
keeps
us apart.
Religion
is how many
wars start.
We need
to figure
out how to love
each other before
we can figure
out the God part!
I am a peaceful being
and we give each other the right
to worship our own way
(as long as neither of us
tries to take God away!)
But really, who has that say?

Money

Money is passed
Back and forth and . . . .
Some overestimate
its worth.

Some think if
they don't have money
they're not fit.
But we don't really own money.
We own what we do for it!

Ownership

My looks, at times, own a collar around your neck.
My eyes own a well, built for me, and you are the water.
My motion owns the most.
My motion owns the world
And the world moves your way as an offering.
My soul sits and waits on Heaven's gift.
My heart owns a mouth
That moves with caution, like a cop.
My future and my past own a mask.
My hope lost a card deal with certainty.
And your eyes brought for me a pedestal,
For my own ownership power all the way
Down to my feet.

The Witness and the Judge

Once I Loved my enemies
but it's futile.
They die from hate, transfixed
by their own sickness.
They told me, "That line that
you won't cross needs just a nudge."
Once I Loved those who were Good too.
But they die also, even with all their fitness!
(All about Heaven, maybe they don't lie.
                    They fudge).
But once upon a time I Loved a boy because,
to my only Love, he was the only witness.
So, who's to judge?

The Dream Man, Less of a Lie

I know me falling in Love
was one sided,
put on by a hunch
or a whim.

And I know the chances
of me catching my dream
man are slim.

Still, I'd rather be existing
in a dream
than be pretending
you're him!

Identity of a Woman

You run your fingers through your hair like,
in my heart, there is the opening of a cage door.
When you say Good-bye, there is the most in my eye.
Oh! What is more?!
The notes in that song change
like a flock of birds changing their flight plan.
Until you, I had lost my identity as a woman,
who flocks to a man.

Maybe

Maybe I don't lose you
    to begin with!
    How can I notice
    if I'm always in bliss?
And maybe when you say "I love you"
it is like a myth.
Maybe I shouldn't get
excited whenever I phone you.
Maybe I think
you are mine
but I'll never own you!
But maybe I don't have you
and maybe you're not mine.
    I don't want
    to face it
    but in the sand
    you drew a line.
    And I can't believe
    I went that far!
    You're not mine!
    I just think you are.

Practical

I'm your opposite because I am a romantic and my head
is in the sky. If you are practical I need advice from you.

Yet I know you can't identify.
You see, I watch the world go by
while you keep it running. I'm just a bard who hides,
full of clever and cunning.
When I chased a boy, I wasn't like you...So down to earth.
I chased a boy who didn't like me. And what's that worth?

I can't be like you anymore, so matter of fact . . . .
I lost my heart to a boy and I can't get it back.
(Maybe you could have done better with him
by all your tact.)
When it comes to men you told me it is realistic for me
to not get my hopes up. And I tried to be real, but with him,
I trust more how he makes me feel.
And sure enough his heart turned out to be fickle.
And then he broke mine in a world I made too magical.
And I see why you choose to be practical.

Time

We have time when we need
Time to know we're secure.

And we have time
For all those certain things we doubt.

I have time before I go to bed
At night to think
Of the way we were.
And we have time when time
Is running out.

When that boy
Left me alone
He cut my heart in halves.

And now I have time
To think
Because time is all I have.

God's Gift Comes to You

Looking toward the future,
I think you could be God's gift to me.
I took matters into my own hands
with the last boy I Loved,
and chased him hopelessly.

And all I got was me running in circles,
caught up in a stare.
Who knows if Life's fair?
A long story short, I got nowhere.

You see, he ran and I ran after him.
But of course, he was too fast and too swift.
That's why I look forward to you,
since now I know,
you don't chase after a gift!

The Criminal

When you ask me yes or no my answer is simple.
But as we get older, simplicity will fade.
And maybe if I just don't hurt anybody,
I've got it made!

That can make me honest
and honest people won't evade.
I loved you and you feel what you feel.
Whatever that is I have to abide.
But whenever you ask me how I feel I'll always
confide. Because free people don't hide!
I'm not scared from the truth in my face!
It is free by the light of the sun.
Years of finding out
who I am
and then showing that
is the only real fun.
And brave people don't run.

Hope

Hope is lovely when you like me.
It delicately takes my hand and
Guides me to you, each time.
Well when you don't like me,
I go to see you, kicking and screaming,
As Hope pulls me by the hair.

Bipolar

I am where my mind is and I hope that is at home.
My friends can't help me if I am lost, then roam.
And then I'll cave, unless I really want to be saved!
And when I am in a good mental state, my mind,
body and soul are brawn.
But where am I whenever that mood is gone?

You Have Power

Angels cannot stop true love.
Neither can demons!
Death cannot stop true love.
But you can!

Covetousness

If you want fame and money without real
Achievement behind it, you're not greedy enough.

What You Do with Your Life

When death comes calling my life is suddenly
So important. But what I do with it isn't??
When life is unimportant, death suddenly is!
Why should I give death power over life?

The Stripper

I see those dignified workers who go home
and use their zipper. Dignity is relative. I was in love
with a stripper. Really the only ones we respect wear
a collar. And I respected that kiss. I got to kiss him
for a dollar. So, you are dignified, right?
Are you telling me my kiss wasn't real? Because
he was too beautiful for me or that I found out
his heart was not a steal? So, if I confess to you,
Oh! Holy Collar,
that I had a real kiss for a dollar,
I have to say, from his stare that will stay,
"That I will follow him, Mister" because
I was in love with a stripper!
And when he is up on that stage angels forget
to age. With more sincerity added with inhibition,
he kissed me
and said "Thank you!" thank you for my time
and my attention. That song must have been
Heaven's rendition! And then the curtain
goes down with sexual danger all around.
Yet he never took part.
He was the first to leave
and always took my heart.
But maybe, when you left the club,
you Loved girls too much! You didn't Love
when they were comfortable in their skin,
but you Love to get under their skin
to touch their hearts, and years later,
when we're still apart since you haven't stayed in touch
I could find you as tired as your act
and then you'll try to leave me waiting again
but first I'll see the Truth and then,
turn my back. The Truth is;
if something is all for show,
how do you find what's True?
When I'm in Love, I say your stage name,
but that's not the same as you!

23

A Fight in Heaven?

I was an angel, to see an angel, and to
Pull away, is to be an angel, and some angels
don't catch you before you fall . . . .

It is lonely up here, where you left me, before
this Battle in Heaven, you see, where you
looked on me. It was simple of me to, like you
then, and I see their backs toward me now,
these angels here, because I won't pull away
anymore, each time, I fall for you, their backs
were turned on a whore for you. And,

Then you backed away too, to see an angel
and pulled away, is to be an angel

And then you love yourself, just a little bit
more, as you climb higher than me, again,
each time, I hope with their help, where time
left you before I fell.

Consummation.

So, know now that we die, and use that in a
cry to me, and I will accept that you will
accept me.

Consummation.

And then I will speak these words with my
cheek to your chest, but careful should I
speak, if you're an angel. And they are
laughing at me now, these many angels here,
telling me what to do with you, So,

I will bring you down to earth, where, angels
cry; This is no young girl's sigh.
Where I can speak to an angel too, and love
you too, with

Consummation.

But this battle will rage with them for you,
because, they don't see that it's for you.

Because, now this is a personal thing and a
person stands alone, when people call
them crazy. And 'who is she' will not be on
your lips anymore.

Because,

Can't we laugh when we are crazy, and can't
we drive when we are crazy, and can't we sigh
when we are crazy, and can't we eat and drink
when we are crazy, in love?

And, who are these people in love? You see,
up here, where you left me,

We don't touch, because;

To pull away is to
Be an angel.

Then they will make you climb higher than
me, I hope and then they will say:

To be an angel, to see an angel, and to pull
away is to be an angel.

And I will tell them, hell! everything's a sin;
To be so high and still to cry. Now that's the
sin. A sin to be an angel and still to see a
human's back so close.

So, he will attack you first, for the worst, all
you angels have ever done.

To keep a human's eyes so closed and an
angel's touch still too delicate to grab.

And you won't get caught by me, I suppose,
since now this is a personal thing, and you,
keep moving in numbers; Lingering, like
death, in numbers.

But when two angels find themselves first,
then won't those numbers burst, fall apart,
then pull away,
Each to be an angel?

South

Where there was only your shoulder
and my weeping eyes.
Did I tell you I made a dead record
come alive?
I need your love and you give me what you can.
But are you hiding the fact that you are a needy
man?
These poems make me elated
then make me blue and I was always
one heartbeat away from getting you.
I go to my window to check my car like I checked
your back so many times
because you usually turn away
and I'm left with an imaginary kiss put in rhymes.
Where a whisper was a scream
and your thigh melted in my mouth.
Where the knives you put in my soul
made my heart go south.

Happy

I smoke until I get lung cancer
From a cigarette.
And that your liver will rot from drinking
Is a good bet. Sex will give you a disease.
Some people think its fun. And oh!
Watch out from getting cancer from too much
Sun! Exercise seems harmless. But you could
Die of course. And a gun could kill me if I leave
My front porch. You can die from too much food.
Plus it makes your arms flappy. After all this,
Wouldn't it be easier to just be happy?

Death

I'm not afraid to go but suffering goes way beyond
my crying.
We are so afraid to die we create something worse
than dying!

Self Sufficient

There was a man who did everything good on his own.
His perfection intimidated others, so he was left all
alone. They could see he needed no help
so if they loved him, he impeded it.
He may have gone to hell because
none of them prayed for him.
They never thought he needed it!

Crazy

The truth is everything
that doesn't hurt a living being, because who says
the truth is only what you're seeing?
Does it really hurt you to let us believe?
You can call me crazy
but there is no truth when you leave.

Crazy

The term 'crazy' should only be applied to people
who are crazy without happiness.

Beaten Down

Trying hard to accomplish something
is complicated.
Just trying is simple.

Violence in the Movies

A gun on someone's mind is sometimes
something you can feel.
When you portray fictional violence to an audience
who doesn't know what is real, it's real!

Not What You See

The Elephant Man was a gentle soul
who scared people.
That was an unjust fear.
But that is probably why
he was scared!

Over Time

I'll prove to you my one accomplishment:
That I can suffer.
And then maybe you'll come to save me . . . .
Only I won't be there!

Final

He steals my heart with the sounds
of orchestra leaves . . . . And then he leaves!

With the speed of a bullet he names my heart
like a shooting star to aim . . . . And then he shoots!

And then he steps on my heart like a monarch
might step to his throne, defiant yet regal,
 We are hurt but not alone!

So, he says "Good-bye" and sees in my eye,
Something crushed like the crest of a wave . . . .
And then, as in the end (unalterable) he waves!

The Dying Soldier

When I look at you,
I guess I think that the order
must have been amiss,
Since any real order
would have been . . .
anything but this!

The Miracle of Life

MY PARENTS

How can I not at least try
to be happy after heartache
from that boy, When their greatest fear
In life is that I won't find joy??
And I learn from this unselfish whim
That their biggest fear is not for them!

WOMEN

I'll never 'have' a man
Until my mind is what he understands.
And what I really 'own' is what attracts him
to me . . . Enhances what I can be!
So, sometimes we search for men with a fling
When the goal is just to be worth something!
Maybe he is not the one to help me do
what I can. My time is my Life.
Look at all we give up to say we have a man!

MY DREAMS

These dreams don't come true
despite what I say.
Am I standing in God's way?
And they won't come true at this rate.
Of all things I know, I was meant to be great!
Yet they move down this timeline
sort-of lyrical.
And what then started in my mind became life,
and that . . . A miracle!

Dark Paw

Did you see the sad skinny cat who
Found the strength to stir
When he saw the pretty one
Being loved and proudly purred?
Please pet me if you will,
Although I'm skinny and I'm sad and
My heart is made of rags.
Please pet me if you can.
I can't persuade you by my looks,
But I'd promise to love you by your hand.

Behind a thin caged door,
Deep down I know a cat can cry.
He forgives me cause he knows
I can't see it in his eyes.
So, if you pet the pretty one
It's much easier to boast.
But still you knew I was the one
Who'd appreciate love the most.

On Sleeping Beauty

Once upon a time two lovers' fear kept them from
saying, "You are mine." Well, how can you be scared
of what you can't keep? Can't keep for how long?
How long can you weep? This fairy tale is all about sleep!
She said, "I like my him and I like his me and, yes, I like
Disney." The question is, "Can you live in a fairy tale?"
Kids taken from this world would wail. Just like a fairy
tale in my heart. How can I fail? For what if death, they
say, was just a spell? And a kiss could break it? Once,
twice, I fell! And a kiss could break it . . . The sender,
to Hell! "For true love conquers all."

But not everyone who has been forbidden in this world
is bad. And maybe a bird can sing the same song I sing,
and if I'm careful, maybe I can have your ring.

In the end, we're all just a witness, to the things we do.
Shop, eat, and fitness too. True love is only how it seems.
You're better off asleep. At least there you can dream.
So in that dream, she was there, at the ball, head up high,
swift and tall, and heard what he said: "True love conquers
all!" She believed in love, so did he, but sometimes their
dreams terrified them, like you and me. And she had seen
this fairy tale before . . . It's those fairies and animals who
brought the magic at the core. And then, once upon a time,
I'll awake and you won't be an animal anymore.

If it wasn't a dream then, can it be a dream now?
The truth is I tried. I loved you and how! And, unlike
her, I wasn't betrothed. I didn't have the wings of the
fairies that clothed. But still, I believe that life can be
a fairy tale.

If you're in Hell, all you can do is fuss. But don't you
want them to know they were wrong about us? And
when your life is hell, dreams tend to be smaller.
You know I won't resist you if you holler.

This princess would foul things up and then put it in rhyme. "No," the fairies said, "You won't mess things up this time." But then Fate said, "This won't end," cause He knows you can't win. And we fall like the sleep that fell on Sleeping Beauty. And pick ourselves up not out of spite but out of duty.
For true love conquers all!

Short Ones

A clear conscience is more important than being alive.

Every time I am stupid Jesus suffers.

Getting close to his skin won't get you
any closer to his morals. And which is he?

Expressing yourself is how people find you.

There is so much time. That is why important things
can't wait.

We would not exist if there wasn't something
we really wanted!

Beyond talent there is a message!

To God every one gift is as important
as every gift.

When you are sleepy you go to sleep.
When you are tired there is nowhere to go.

I am all alone but I can still be counted on.
I am all alone but I can still be there for
people!

Sometimes to catch a star you must release
a tear. And to remember a dream you must
forget a fear.

The truth is everything that doesn't hurt
a living being.

I don't see how people can say they love
their bodies and still go out and be
promiscuous.

Jesus, What's Fair?

I speak of love
But they will fight.
I'm here to deliver us from evil
But they will fight.
My kingdom is in heaven
But they will fight.
I choose not to fight
But they will fight.
I thought I loved my Father the most
But they will fight.
Then we choose not to understand
And with a heart filled
By persecution– ask them why?
And what did he fight?
Hypocrisy
Jealousy
Fear
Intimidation
Cowardice
And evil.
Do you believe he rose on the third day?
Peter– is all I have to say.

Jesus said, "I suffered for your sins, yours and such."
And I replied, "I'm not worth that much!"

"I suffered for your sins.
 Don't worry! I will rise again!
 If you believe me, tell my story to men."

And I replied:
        "What a cost! . . .
To not be lost,
And what a cost to be free.
 In a way your suffering still hurts me."

And Jesus said, "One time I fell,
And my mother was there,
Just like you too.

And just for you,
I suffered to make new."

    So if I tell the story, my way,
    That one day,
    The man responsible for the crucifixion
    Will suffer by destiny
    From a death made of fiction.

My wounds start in my head.
"Love your enemies," the Bible said.
My wounds make it hard to forgive.
But I do what I can to learn how to live.
I endure wounds and sores and
in your heart my wounds add to yours.
But for your sake my wounds are healed.
And now that I think about it,
Many times I've kneeled,
When my dreams for you make a promise sealed!

Life and Death

When I create and give back,
I Love and there is always just enough for me to take.
If I'm alive, passion for Life can't be a mistake.
And God, for whatever reason, ... He never lied!
When I go to die, I'll be greedy and satisfied.

Faith in People

You think. So if the bad man wins, he won on your whim.
Nobody has power over you unless you give it to them.
Sometimes you must stand to think
And I might find you all alone.
If you give that boy power over you, he must face you,
as long as you have a mind of your own.

Happiness

Moments we face
Moments we chase
Moments that plead our case.

Moments we choose
Moments we lose
Moments from God we abuse.

Moments that fly
Moments so high
Moments I swear I can pull from the sky!

Moments the weak will lack
Moments the strong will attack
And oh! Moments that I want back.

My Meaning of Life

I. The Wounds of Time

Even though I am hurting, I still have to pay for my sins.
God made my heart so delicate, but, after this world is done,
we have grown such thick skins, With such gaping wounds
from this Life . . . . . . So, who wins?
I Loved a boy and our Love for one another
could have set an example for others,
and shown them where to start,
but they would all just be a mime,
and if our Love has made art, this suffering will die
because it is on borrowed time.
Time is truly the last test. But the question is this;
Can time truly heal the heartache in my chest?

II. Fate

I have the Love from these Love poems written years ago
By all these bards. Yet being able to find our True Love
was not in the cards. They have cast the first stone
and I see we stone them, but once my Love gets out,
I won't rely on the cards. I'll own them!

III.

God put me down here to Live, yet Life pushes me below
and below. But its meaning will always be right above,
and, if I'm lucky, I learn resilience, tenacity and Love.

My friends were my enemies and when I'm down,
they choose to be gone.
But unlikely they know I continue to find
my Life's fulfillment. Unlikely they know,
but I've moved on, to a Life where I find,
I'm much more resilient.

When I don't remember all those years I waited,
when I have no memory of those mistakes I've dated,
only what I've Loved and what I've hated,
it must be Fated to be on this path God will govern,
and I simply stay with Him because I'm so stubborn.
When everyone wants me gone, what kills me is,
I can't remember my chastity, Yet with God,
I will go on and on, because I stay with Him
by my tenacity.

If someone were to ask me my meaning of Life,
a picture of you would pop into my head even before I blink.
And, in this Life, ultimately, you have to care
before you think. And, in this world,
everything is measured relatively
(except dreaming of you,
so light and breezy.)
The meaning of Life is when I Love you worthwhile,
sometimes it's not even easy.
Usually the harder it is to get you to Love me,
the easier it is to Love you (or I give up and leave you be),
is when I find out, you're much too good for me!

Aging Actress

Why don't you give up glamour for reality?
All those surgical procedures; just throw them away!
Exercise less than ten times a week, eat pizza
and let your hair go gray.
               I mean, would that make you ugly?
You can pretend you are in charge of your hair,
your face and your bod.
But no one controls Mother Nature and God.
Because maybe you relied too much on your looks
getting famous. I guess back then that's how it was.
But now I'm here and I say that you will still be beautiful
no matter what the celebrity buzz,
since God may see us differently
than "Vogue Magazine" does!

Greedy

Time stands still with him
When everything he does flatters.
And every minute counts, not because it ends
But because it matters!

You Can Make Someone Like You

The truth is when you don't like me,
I just don't understand. How do I discern?
Maybe if you knew more about me!
Wouldn't you love me then, the more you learn?
I mean, can't you see me?
Can't you hear me?
Can't you feel me?
I do exist now, don't I?
Like me not for who I am!
But who I can be.
Are you scared I won't like you?
Be yourself! I dare you to show me.
And if you don't love me,
That's because you don't know me.
I'll try to make you like me to the death.
Don't you admire my perseverance
down to my very last breath?
And to get rid of me, you have to know my psychology.
My mind is full of fairy tales.
But the truth distorts.
A prince loves a princess, who he adores and he courts.
That secret I hold inside comes out in spurts.
And my will to get you to like me tries so hard it hurts!

I tell my own story where someone grows
Into becoming Divine.
Humility is a good place to start.
You have to like me because you don't know
What I go through when we're apart.
Would you like me better if you knew I was
After everyone's heart?

The very thing that keeps me attracted to you
And keeps me fearless when I address you,
Is the fact that I keep failing to impress you.

Maybe it is a death wish to force love on you.
All the while I'm a bombarder.
If someone tells me I'll never win,
I say to myself "Try harder!"
And you outshine all the others with your morals.
And you are kind. That too.
I don't like "men" without a particular man in mind.
And that's you! We are influenced by our friends
And magazines, T.V. and authorities.
We are influenced by majorities. And least of all, Love.
You feel Love when Fate decides that it should strike you.
So then, why can't I ask that you be persuaded to say,
"I like you!"?

The Old Dream

Youth is a car sale. The salesman lies.
But we get one look at it and it's sold.
So why did the angels give me this dream now,
when I'm old?
My dream was too old and now I'm too old for my dream!
With a dream comes comfort.
We rest our heads easy on our thoughts,
pillow soft ....
I believe, when I was young, I could have pulled it off!

I Live and prosper only
in the part of my mind you understand.

These Evil Thoughts

I go to a shrink to figure out how the world thinks.
But in that world, where's me?
And there, I tell him, my own mind scares me!
This world wants to take me and produce a lovely lady.
But I go to him because we keep inside all that's shady.

Does God expect me to be benevolent
because Someone says I should?
I will desire that on my own !
That evil thought relieves the pressure on me
to be Good when I'm alone.
I must have that feeling of Goodness on my own.
And maybe that feeling would be true.
But those creepy, evil thoughts lead me somewhere
without you. I think my heart is true.
But in my mind is corruption.
You think I got over that boy.
But I only got over him
just enough to function.

These sacrilegious thoughts have nothing to do
with religion at all! Or what religion could be!
They're just all about me, and the Bible I never move
from the shelf. A sacrilegious thought is just me
hurting myself. And it's result? Is me feeling morose.
I find religion that close!

So, maybe all these evil thoughts are lies.
Lies that don't stem from my heart,
which could be of use. But from a society
who puts no value on being wise. Those evil thoughts!
I guess there is no excuse.

So, God is here and I am the captain of my ship.
Which One of us drives it? With that in mind,
how painful it is to let you in on these evil thoughts
so private!

Helpless

We don't make a choice to fall
In Love. That is something that
Just happened to me!
I told you I Love you.
And since it was one-sided
That continues to amuse you.
But I never had you, so, how can I lose you?
God chose for me the man of my dreams.
But His warning to me was: "If he doesn't like you,
Fate will abuse you!"
So, I may have chased you.
But I didn't choose you!

Spirit

I was thinking of taking my life when I saw a proud person
Standing next to me. I thought I had nothing to live for
But this person lived and he had less than me!
Throughout my life I look at what I never had
And throughout that time I've ranted.
Even though I have more, he appreciates the shoes he's in
And takes nothing for granted.
He was standing next to me with such gratitude
I felt near it.
To stop me from taking my life he loved his and,
In essence, gave me spirit!

Faith

When you tell me you are leaving I will get on with my life . . .
Well, I may!
I hope it wasn't me that made you leave! But if it wasn't
You would stay.
I bet faith would be easy if I had any kind of a say!

This Dream of You

My dream crumbled once I realized you and I
were not mutual.
The "no" you said rumbled in my ears. With all my pain,
You remain neutral.
But this smile tumbled when my dream of you
Became so crucial!

Everytime

My happiness may be selfish but my misery is a crime.
I'm lucky to have so many people to mime.
When I am surrounded by love but still find myself sad,
I wished I had a dime . . . .
The time of your life should be everytime!

Youth Cries

Youth is like a car sale. The salesman lies.
But we see it and it's sold.
If, as I mature, I forget my happiness,
I don't want dry eyes when I get old.

He Who is Without Sin

I chased this boy and, instead of liking me,
He cast a stone and I was out.
If Love is a crime, we have no control
Of it's punishment, which leaves me with doubt.
But I'm not even concerned with 'his' sins.
I've got my own to worry about!

Forgetting Life

You run to the jester to laugh,
And to forget the worries that pain you.
That jester split your gut in half,
But Life Itself is not here to entertain you!

The Church

I practice in my head over and over this play for you.
You sit in the back row but I want you so close
you feel my history.
My play is a triumph but a tragedy and mainly, a mystery.
You see, I'm nervous because I know
the distance in the theatre
and each time, you are my audition.
Every word of Love I say that doesn't make it
to the back row has its own rendition.
Unlike make believe, my play has no end.
But she is on your mind and when I see you again,
mine is gone with the wind.
In the back row I know she may always lurch.
So just know my play, which says that Love is a church.

What They Will Think in the End

If the point of my Life was to have people
going to their graves thinking I'm great,
maybe I did nothing for their sake.
        In essence, I take.
        But if I have them going to their graves
thinking THEY"RE great, by my prayer or by a plea,
then I may believe the same about me!

Interest over Pain

After heartache from that boy,
I felt like I had barely survived a war.
All I cared about was, "How can I suffer more?"
But when you look at me . . . . The suffering?
Nevermind!! Since you are only interested in
what is on my mind.

Humanity

Eventually every dreamer dreams his heart is resting
Peacefully by a steeple.
I've seen heroes who have blown my hair back.
I just watch being that I am so feeble.
If your dream just won't come True, try trusting people!

Learn on My Own

When I grow up I own something no one bought me.
I learn when I know something they never taught me.
And I think something on my own.
Learning Trust (that you can learn) is bigger
than some information.
They don't have to help me now (but I'm not alone).

The Lovers, Not the Fighters

Although we've never fought, you and my gift to you
Were arm wrestling each other for my survival.
I didn't know what you thought of me.
You must be thinking of another rival.
And although my gift of Love is bigger than you,
You won because you can't force Love on anyone.
And when you won't let me Love, aren't I the peaceful one?

Misfortune

If the whole world is not about me then, why me?
Ultimately, I guess, see if I care!
But when it comes to the aspects of my heart,
I'm allowed to declare: 'fair' and 'unfair'.

Out of My League

In my mind, I mind you and in my dream,
I always floor you.
And, when you pop into my head, how do I ignore you?
I told my friends I liked you . . . . They laughed
and said, "What will be will be.
But you know there are many more fish in the sea".
Well, in that sea, I can't even get the worst.
So I allow myself to go after the best.
I allow myself to think I'm good enough
to have your tender heart.
On me though, your external beauty is tough,
And if for once my head hangs down,
my spirit says, "Look up!"
Beauty on the inside. Beauty on the outside. . . . .
and I know so much that I don't know anymore
what's True. Because you are so vulnerable sometimes,
you're more than even you.
And when I told my friends I liked you, they said,
"Can't you lower the bar a little and like someone else?"
But they didn't know; Loving you means
I think highly of myself.

Finding a Job

Don't think about money.
First think about your Time.
You have to Love what you do because what you do
Is your Life, not the money.
Then think about your passion.
That is where you should find your job.

Where is Death

When they want us to forget our faith,
they'll say that the idea of Heaven is us just fishing.
Is death what I feel or what they'll feel when I'm missing?
Is death only here when I'm in pieces or, in a whole,
am I still a part? Does death start in the heart?
How unfair it is that death is what I look forward
to after living with so much strife!
If we're not careful, death begins in Life!

Hanging on Too Long

I said, "I Love you", and you look so stern,
do you Love me back?
You didn't even have to say "No!"
No matter how I Live or what I learn,
the heartache you gave me is what I know!

Now and Then

Now, when you can see a kiss, naked and bare,
but reality says then, "It's not really there!",
you dream from your heart, True,
until the future is fair.
You see, it gets harder and harder the more I care!
Because the consequences are real, where real dreamers
don't win and my heart being True felt no reward,
I Love men. Maybe there is no reward, no reward
without you, until any, little gift from God I hoard . . . . . .
but where Life is unfair is where I've been.
My Lover can't Love me now, but he says, "Until then!"

The Other One

The way you felt was real without his tampering
and you do nothing wrong in the way things
are happening. Yet he Loved to punish you
before the Truth was Who you served.
He said that he Loved you, but when it came to showing it,
he never had the nerve.
Now you Love another who appreciates your humility
and you appreciate him, reserved.
Wouldn't you Love to tell him that finally,
someone got what they deserved?

In Awe of Myself

When I Loved you, and faced all the cost,
it's not the hope you gave.
It's the faith, when all hope is lost!
I Loved you at first, for shallowness and despite brevity.
but what continues to put me at awe is Love's persistence
and longevity.

All or Nothing

I came from nothing, yet in my mind
I had something that would impress.
It may have took nothing less
To achieve all from nothing, I confess.
In the face of reality, I have a dream and I adore it.
Maybe all is all only if I've sacrificed for it.
And for each step I take, I have to climb a wall.
Maybe I had more than nothing to offer after all!

The Slut

You misunderstood me because I don't want
To have sex with anyone. Only when my feelings are True.
Before you even knew who I was, I chose you!
Maybe it's a sin to be near you and just want more.
Maybe with what I'm feeling,
I can't look down on any whore.
If sex can be a gift from the heart,
maybe no other man will do.
And yes! I am a slut. But only for you.

Alone

Without being able to be alone with you, I just want to be
Alone. But when I'm alone with you, I'm:
Alone below the line we'll never cross.
Alone with you as a payoff for the prayers I've said under a
Cross,
Alone, hearing one word you say for me to forget fear.
Alone with you, pulling me from alone with a tear.
Alone with you above the clouds.
Alone with you in the middle of the crowds.
Alone with my determination for you and all your charms.
Alone in your arms.
Alone with you in any room in the world I can find.
And me! Alone on your mind.
Alone with you (Got to remember a lonely past!)
And alone with you. Alone at last!

The Dream and the Conscience

Some people Live their dream. I Live in want of a dream.
But all of us wake up in the morning and we are back
in the saddles. We choose our battles, by what we conceive.
Some dreams are so hard to achieve!
If they won't come True,
I feel I'm being punished.
When the world revolves around me, that's how it seems.
There is a battle for our conscience and a battle
for our dreams. One time you made me feel special.
I never can figure out when you bluff!
Maybe with the question of my dream . . . .
well, I'm a Good person. Isn't that enough?

Reflection

When I'm with him and I'm nervous and I don't know
what I'm saying, it's possible that I'm wooing.
And when I'm alone, trying to figure out the world
and thoughts go back to him, it's possible I Love
to be stewing. So, of all things possible, isn't it possible
I'm doing better than I think I'm doing?

Please

Maybe in this Life I've reached my height and now
I'm on the way down. There are no more fish in the sea
when you don't feel and you drown.
When the courageous can no longer fly,
are they still called "birds"?
When I say, "I Love you", please take it!
Since all I have left are the words.

Where I Find My Happiness

They laughed at me for finding joy from my Good,
absurd dream. So I tell them that my Good feelings
are as real as they seem.
Wouldn't it be boring
if everyone didn't march to the beat of their own drum?
I'll tell you, if I'm happy, does it really matter where
that comes from?

Mind Over Matter

I Love you but all your success makes me nervous
and your charms, they just scratch below the surface.
While a youthful spirit, everyday, soars in the skies . . . .
You are the 'youthful' behind those aged eyes!
How do you stay youthful? Well, you pay attention
to all the Love songs we've sung, where I'm tired
of complex and I just want kind. You're old but we look
at you and see 'young', because it all starts in your mind!

When's the Rescue?

I was counting on you to come and save the day,
but there are so many days!

The Illusion of an Insult

When I was young, my first boyfriend called me "useless"
and became a rival. Over the years, I've been made useful
by my own survival. So he called me some useless thing
to be where I'm at. But he doesn't believe his own insult.
He wants me to believe that!

Don't Ask, Don't Tell

If anybody cared to wonder who I Loved most
in the world I'd tell them it was you.
But my crush is a secret that makes me blue.
And getting over you, I would say to them,
is the hardest task . . . . . But no one asked!
I don't know yet the secret to being a brave person.
And as I get older, my fear worsens.
The longer I go without you, without you is more certain.
And the more I learn from them, the more I believe
there is a mystery on how to put you in my future
they're selling . . . . . . But no one is telling!

For Me, For You, For the World

I say the words, "I Love you", before I speak.
And I stay before I'm invited. I worship your humility
with all my ability. When you are real,
I can touch you, the Untouchable.
When there is the world, I protect myself.
When there is you, I feel selfish . . . .
But how much of that is me?

The Sad Dog

My Life boils down to what I want,
what I have and what I had.
No matter how long I Live,
I can't shake what makes me sad.
As a child, if someone hurt me, I would distract myself
and squirm and fiddle.
When I was young, sadness followed me
like a puppy dog because I was so little.
Looking back, I never wallowed,
but somehow sadness followed.
So as a teenager, I became a little worse.
As a young person, we never follow our own course.
A stray dog of sadness made me roam when I left home.
My sad dog tells me, "A glass half empty never fills me."
And then I was alone where my sadness was an attack dog,
and he kills me. No matter how hard we try,
we can't see the tears in a sad dog's eyes.
Maybe, in old age, sadness is my seeing eye dog
and warns me where worse sadness lies!
I've learned that a cat has nine Lives.
It feels like my sad dog has a million and seven!
If sadness took my Life, can someone who led a dog's life
go to Heaven?

The Faith and the Heart

The Goodness they taught me. . . . . . When I am born,
I believe it! And my faith? It was inconceivable
that I would ever leave it. But if I do,
I must rely on what I have or just what I can conceive.
So I'll do what I always do . . . . .
Wear my heart on my sleeve.

Heaven and Earth

You say you want to go to Heaven but it is for the elite
who say the magic word, pay the price
and know the secret password. God doesn't just Love you.
He bends over backward.
You can say you like someone, and is that all?
With those words, what's that worth?
God doesn't just like you! He moves Heaven and earth.

Ironic Love

You just don't care but I can't understand
that my chances are slim.
The less interested you are in me,
the more in Love I am.

Cover My Eyes

If I could go through my adult Life like a child,
protected from suffering, protected from seeing it,
everyone would be jealous because I would be special,
like a child. Like a child.
The rights of children are our rights.
At the movies, why doesn't he cover my eyes
where there are gun fights, or when the vampire bites,
or when Lovers sin all night, or when a wise man
loses his sight, or when, well, morals are trite?
Suffering may never go away, but Life, we will preserve it.
The first step in creating your mind's utopia
is knowing you deserve it!

The Word of Magic

Words come from the heart, extravagant and simple . . . . .
Words after you could build by pain a temple.
Words of everyday Life become bricks to a story
of romance made tragic. Words made by your ear,
the word I call, "Magic". What do they mean?
They mean more than "How are you doing? I'm fine!"
Simple. My word of "magic" means you're mine
(and no less!). You say, "Stay!" and I say, "Yes!"

Depending on Where My Mind Is

There is a fine line between comedy and tragedy.
With comedy, your heart heeds to laughter in and around
and between others. In tragedy, your heart bleeds for,
before and after one another. With comedy,
you can forget your problems, and fast.
Unfortunately, it always seems it's the tragedy that lasts!

Punish

I know if I am punished, what will be taken from me
is something I Love. The more things I Love, the harder
it is to punish me!

Your Hands

I try to push you into Love with me, but you always fold,
relentlessly. All my Life, your rejection lingers.
You could have tried to hold onto me but I slipped
through your fingers. I want to be a better person
and you are there to give me 'thumbs up'.
But that is just in my head, that you're there,
so I try nothing and my numb disrupts.
You said once, "I Love you", which was a con.
Like when a false fortune teller reads your palm.
(Your eyes and demeanor were always like an ocean
when it's calm.) Mostly, in Life, I'm in the dark,
until your hands are on me. To a blind person,
it's your hands that see! We use hands to speak, read,
write and pray. Your heart shows in your hands.
My heart is in your hands. So I obey.

Buying Good

You sell me you're Good and I bought it!
Every time, I learn and you taught it.
Taught it for you to be so Good I could try it.
And then, you tell me I'm Good and I buy it.

The Chase of the Brick Wall

When I chased that boy, I was so dumb!
I chased him blissfully and senselessly.
But it wasn't meant to be . . . . . I know this
because, God was chasing me, relentlessly.

If You're Lost

They say, "Move it or lose it!" but the hares
never win the race. It's always the turtles!
When I'm lost, I panic when I can't find you
and I run in circles. I've spent my whole Life trying
to figure out 'who is me?' And in the afterLife,
that's who I'll be . . . . . Still me!
So maybe when I die, I'll go to a star, And they won't say,
"Move." They'll say, "You've made it this far!"
In a dream when I am running and
you're running behind me,
we lose our wind and our will.
When I'm lost and I want you to find me,
I won't run in circles. I'll stay still like you've taught,
stay still like that still thought.

Dustin Pickering

Angels in the Dark

for Audrey

If in this softly focused night,
for naught I kiss your eyes
as stars emblazon your curious smile:
what instance brings me to you
as a servant of the sound?

Do I seek fathomless swords of your kiss
and do I drown in the sea of compunction
as I lose my thoughts in your perfect form?

Let the language of my trust
frame my tenderness as nothing less
than love's sweet tongue.
Your flowing song as breath in natural voice
delights each heart,
yet you know as the darkness encroaches
my own thoughts are on you.
I reach to read the heart you bear to me.

Something of passion is here,
listening. I cannot let it go
because it holds me in silence.
I had hopes placed in those lips
that form the most measureless magic
of your smile;
I wanted to kiss them and hear them
tell me what the world imparts.
However, my heart will not stop its ache
and you cannot stop it even
if language could cry for me
as I try, again, in these words
to tell you my heart cannot leave.

The Most of Your Glory

I cannot...
the opposition is too strong.
Your face glows in the summer heat
while your purple dress clings to your body.
You are made to the night
and the fact you will never love me...
innocent is a desperate cry from the good
who never receive.

Some part of me loves you for its own sake
because you are beautiful,
and the most of your glory is hidden in the heart.
Voice reaching out past the enigmas of motion,
I pull you in like a sword of suicide.
You stand and make a silent face
while my torch of incense bears the burden of tribute.

She Is Only the Truth

I cannot object to the conscience
I am presented with,
this nightcap caving in and loosening my eyes.

I gravitate to the yearning of all being.
Her name knows this, and she is only the truth.
No lie can exist in her heart,
and because of this I cannot have her.
I lie. I am a graceful icon.
My sharp arrows of fire
govern the sarcasm of her smile.

I know only what I am told to know.
I know nothing at all.
The last emptiness of my touch,
where I hide my mystic torch,
is the conqueror conjuring the brightness.

I pass a last moment to you
while you look into the mirror
heightened by your shiver...
the last thought cancels the edge
where I fall and singe my glance.

Where Are You?

I am not surprised at your nod.
You ask me to move forward
but like an angel in doubt
I hide my stolen fares.
Whisper in splendor,
I carry you in my old age
like a ring.
Fire is a majestic thing.
I cannot worry about you in faith
but I see you in the dark
wanting to be the light,
asking for a touch,
holding the bliss of symposium
in your cautious glass.

It's not the mirror that mocks.
Something in the soul bites.
Ice hits the wind and the scream
of hideous masks removed
makes the burns insoluble.

I open your letter for the last time.
The words have disappeared.
I don't know where you are.
I couldn't have lost you...
where are you?

Every time I die
my heart speaks your name
as if to breathe truth
in the dark.

for e.b.

your language is a galloping horse,
fleeing wind of violence with vigilance,
lost in curtains of dream
where sun warms the old secrets
of time on Holden Caulfield Beach.
i am perplexed by your stars, your mischief.

young devil, let my soul consume the
stone of child's play like a grain
in a bird's mouth.

i have usurped your river of thought
and looked up words in your dictionary
without your permission.   your gray
face is a winter escalator to the beads
of time one day you shall consume.

for e.b. #2

she walks as callous as a broken shell
knowing never doom
and making paint breathe
the magic of love.

love disappears when the heart
chokes on sublime species
and special hours
I am drawn into this dreamy
young Michelangelo
while she remembers crossing
the river of second chances.

i can't look a gifted horse
in the eye without tears
and empty spirits becoming livid
with rage.

how does the mare toss back her plural
heart—   and see no light?

for e. b. #3
elucidation

i look to the poetry of youth
rising, the young artists
dreaming,
to know the future of the world.

elena   — a poem, please?
you kiss language, and
let its free fires fluster and smother
to bite wisdom in its fearful grip.

do you know all truth is fire
and your drawings burn my
stained eyes with pleasure and dream?

your playful gallop, dog's laugh
in sturdy fear: rhythm and spirit!
elena, a poem please?

I Think of Love

My eyes, sharp as a cat's and purring
with the fondness of pride—
when I gaze into another's,
I find semblances of hope.

Moment assassinates moment—
like a true murderer of Being,
Time clutches heavy bodies and disappears.

I am indifferent-- I think of love.

Impressions

Can love be mathematical?
Some reduce sabbatical--
yet when one and one come together,
they remain as one in fresh daylight.
They leave impressions on sand
and even though the waves take all back,
they become one with the source
of our longing and being.

Popcorn

The world is beside me.
I could stride a river's currents
And float like a veil. Magic.
My head full of romantic air,
Buttery sweet like popcorn,
I gaze like a bird
Into the nest of desire.
I do not pluck rose petals
For love. Instead I drop kernels
On my sweater and count them.

If Happiness

If happiness is transmitted to and fro,
visualized waves turn particle
and bounce like moonbeams.
My smile contains lost image--
your quantum dream is parleyed
to my ear. I am silent.
Your eye holds pure fantasy
in a realm of awakening.
I am listless like a willow.

The Fall

I would kiss...something, but your glance
Is a peeled onion. I am no fox of the wood
Taking the pleasure from a hawk.
I have fallen into disrepute for your touch only.
Was the fall worth it? I was caught in cat's cradle
Of windless trees. My arms strung high as kites.
You weren't me in my seeking. I wanted sleep.
Instead I got a dream.

Wishbone Heart

If I present my heart,
each moment will break in two
like a wishbone.
After all, it is mine and yours.
I stand strong to show
how we've hurt one another
in the perfect light.
I don't ask for anything
but the stillness I present
in this image of forgiveness.

Mercy speaks.

Opens

I've talked my love woes till they turned grey;
scarlet hues last not through one day.
My heart opens like a wondrous sea
and floods the horizon with thoughts of me.

The night swallows my pain like a beast
putting to art that delicate feast.
My lady approaches like a ship at noon
sailing through the crimson room.

Her eyes convey deep desire
during my innocence of empire.
Our lusts in embrace turn cities to ash.
War of the flesh marries in the last.

Yet vain hopes are all I have held.
Her breasts so lush were vanity revealed.

Four Reasons You Should Love Me

Like a compass I am steady.
The night sullenly directs like a waltz.
Dreamtime interrupts like fears fantastic.
I will not make unrequited vows.

You are yellow in your ways.
Not a coward but the pulse of a beam.
Light curried to its solitude.
I don't speak when not spoken to.

Because you love me but do not tell,
I keep a stormy eye on your tempers.
The needle drifts and an abuse sets in.
I know how to fight like a man.

If they come to you with swords and shadows,
my heart will protect your body with flames.
I am the cherub at Immortality's hub.
I know who I love is the source of sacredness.

I will not make unrequited vows
unless my love rests committed as an art.
I won't speak when not spoken to
because silence is a gift to the wise.
I know how to fight like a man
but I must only guard your sleeping eyes.
I know who I love is the source of sacredness.

Fear's Gallows
for M. S.

The face stares with cotton candy brevity, licked clean as a straw. Something in the air conspires to imprison chariots of mastery. I return the eyes like sparks of winter. Winds challenge love in fear's gallows while I, a miscreant, seek subtle disarray. I am criminal on the path of subterfuge but my heart intends to remain pure. Something ancient stirs these graces; archaic remnants foster the plows in afternoon's fields. I want the surprise to remain anonymous. You are like a final rose on death's own coffin. She slept and I wept, carrying the crosses of tears to your chalice. I have never known love with this stark radiance, but the eagle is your work widening the gates of lust while torpor inflames your image.

When your sweet dreams linger long with afterglow, you will fly like a courtesan of rain through the mysterious sky. Ambivalence is my secret ghost—he tangles your lips with metaphor. The Magi are hopeless in their search for silence. At night, you are a shining star that knows the source of light.

Still Deep

Held tight by
flesh's desperation,
my love whispers in
cataclysmic darkness,
to me,
"How can we see, together,
with one plasmic eye,
tenderly unknowing and blank,
what the forest fears to tell?"

Now the hard, stiff blade
of autonomy
plunges at my throat. I say,
"No, no. We are still deep."

**on the tenderness of those who remain
unknown to one another**

now we watch, faithfully,
this origin come closer:
it is as if we are giving birth
one to the other,
you the icon of my touch
and i, your magic heirloom.

i gaze as a crystal gazes
in a cave of love and dying.
together, we are the fossils of passions
we once had
and hid in the earth,
sea upturning and cleansing.
we are slowly, if hypnotically,
becoming one another
in this lovemaking, this touch and fever:
we are children slowly being born
in each other's arms.

we long for the eyes of another.
we hold, we kiss, the rain comes like soft tears.
i have never seen you, not in the pulp of contact,
yet in some surreal way I make you vulnerable.
you remember the prisms that captivated you in youth.
you blow me kisses and our love is sealed with the grandeur
of a poem.
whose poem?

Love, Love, Love

Where can two hands meet?
In the hour of masks,
when the square becomes
the circle,
as we brood in the dark.

Two hands meet through common yearning.
We are fortuitous in our freedom.
There is a position for the body
that brings the wino's eyes.
We are drunk on the wine of confusion.
Sweet, tender mercy! Do we know of death?

Golden awareness, the bandage
over my eyes that permits a vision of my existence:
love, love, love.

Reasons

Reasons, there are reasons
I am sold to silence
and enslaved to prophecy's tears.

Reasons I cannot understand.
Reasons I surrender
to the desires of my heart
and shatter the tablets of stone.

Broken artifice of Time,
broken gestures of democracy,
let the morning come!
Let it come to dream of fire and salt.

I Need Someone to Cease My Soul Tears
to A.N.C.

When she thinks,
I understand.
While she is grace,
I command.
Where she sees,
I will also be.

I need someone to cease my soul tears.
That specter has cried for decades.
I've let the rivers flow
until they met in the center of the garden.

O Eden: once paradise proclaimed
the heart as the navel of emotion,
I knew love existed
--just not for me.

Then my sullen sulking drew its bright sword
and light flooded my eyes.
I saw the world as pure perfection in disguise.
The words of conversationalists became meaningful.

You, the one I cried for and sought in desperate dreaming,
make my lamp grow brighter.
From each person I sensed uniqueness
after your gaze reached my eyes.

All the world is veiled in dark peace
until its scars are removed.
Magic love, a deacon of old wisdom—
O, make her come alive!

She knows me and I have
talked to her for years unknowingly—
always honestly.
She is my spirit animal and earthly desire.

Her totem becomes my living art,
and each door is closed
but I sense the Life opening like a dream.
(O, make her come alive!)

My soul tears ceased in the darkness of the fiery night
as sharp scalpels remove my murderous impulses.
Although, I only fault my heart
for approaching too early a depth it could not comprehend.

I will no longer cry in my soul.
She is alive, beautifully alive—
and our masks are bravely shorn, piece by piece.

Kisses

What good do these kisses do,
stretched by sidelong glance
and empty fire?
Do ashes, enraptured by
a cunning smart,
quest forward and dig through
eternal rage?

My essence is of fire,
my heart is a bitter worm
seeking depth— straightened like arrow
before the smiles of doom.
Yet none may know of the cycle of blood
in the trove of chaos,
dreaming of fear?

The midnight teems over my veins,
sullenly pressing its teeth through my wistful eyes—
do I know the shunned one
and do I forsake the outcast?
Harbor now the trust of one who is beautiful.
The instance of affection is mere paradox.

My veins spin the blood like fire
and envy do I hold as lover fair—
do my kisses smart lips of gold,
my own flustering, and dream bold as iron?

They Won't Forget to Pray
verses in response to "So Long Marianne"

In the night,
you asked for silence
to speak to angels
for Marianne, for Marianne.

You opened your lips
and dry as they were still breathed
the confession of stillness.
Darkness approached as you addressed
love in its trembling thoughts.

I can't hear your voice.
It is quiet and the world continues to echo
the room you left empty when you died.
If there was anything left,
it was a pipe and a small notebook with scribbles.

Oh, Marianne has left the stage in hours before.
Her heavenly corpse stills the wind in wonder
like a Scripture of earth and sea.
She is by your side in the winter
while your face is quiet in tears.

SING.

i will wait
for my eyebeams to clear
the night,
as soft as a spoken storm

brows- we know nothing
behind outhouses
that become our brains

dispose the dispossessed fragment

wait, a sudden flesh
coming near

to the bright cave of fantasy
her immortal inamorata returns, misconstrued

yet fully open to the decade
when my heart pumped its gravity
into the chilling bone

i see the dark, displaced

silver spoon of centuries
let my earth be built-
and i will break the eternity

of my heart.

I crave the cavern where i spooned
the craven duress of monks
like ashes and liberation
from one tunnel or another
my laughter will be heard

SING

On Voluntary Hope

Jewels are hidden under light.
In the core of this dream
   lingers the greenest naiveté.
Our eyes are focused for surreal abandon.
We sleep in the eternal musk
   of closing hands, letting go
   of our silence.
Sing to obey the light.
Jewels hang under voices.
The light lingers like fresh lilies
   but tomorrow will come,
   if we only harvest our gifts.

Break My Heart Again

Break my heart again, my dear One
who fears the false world.
Uproot my tree and trek my angel wings.

My solitude, you flutter now,
on my wings—
the heart stutters to shed tears.

Jealousy, wrath, *Da,* and the life
I have lived
malodorously in the forest's shadows.

What are your thoughts, playful One?
My envy strikes like lightning
and soon I am playing with fire.

Do you miss the smiles I gave
and does the wind
still hold my kiss?

Was my letter mailed with dark wish
mysterious?
Why do Poets know all, bear all?

o Beauty, stop:
rid me of myself.
I am feckless in the streets, yearning.

My heart sinks, floats, rises in the poem.
Yearning, a kiss of fires malcontent,
gave my All the absence of wings.

Alas!

"Time is a game
played beautifully
by children."
— Heraclitus, Fragment 79

Jazz of my soul, kindly direct me
to the street
where children play without bruising

their seasons strong.
Stag. Glorious drifter, and let my heart
wreck the gloom.

I waited in the horror, bent by curious wings:
o heart, stop, death is love's wakening.
Stop, kill me, and let the sin grow stronger.

Alas! I am dead.
Mourn me with the violence of the altar:
through me, seek to yearn.

Ideas flood my valleys; my anchorage
keeps the miller content.
Carefully choosing my words,
passion kills 'till I cry.

Lift me now in the dying shroud.
Kiss me as You wouldn't before.
The lyrical dance, o mysterious soul,
will hurt less now.

Together we have played someone else's game.
Why do the readers care
if we love, unaware that depths are pouring out?

Shivers, dense and determined, will release my ecstasy.
Fire, break the pact.
Come nearer, Sasha—
touch me, let's not forget.

Love, shudder and face me

Love, shudder and face me:
look at these cold, keen eyes
and terrify them.
Make sound into light
and drive each fault down harder into my heart.

I am numb with confusion
and this madness makes me inept
at revealing my truth...
at seeing the beauty
or knowing its service to my lies.

If love is penultimate whisper,
it must show itself at the end of time
and not come to the edge of the pool,
waiting for the instant of sinking.

I become numb as the Novocain of my heart
flows through my anticipation...
every dream, every thought,
usurped by her bountiful eyes
looking at me,
exposing my darkest graces.

Wheels of fire and desire

Wheels of fire and desire
turn and shake through the glass
while the magic lifts and fades.
Her sweetness remains.
I cannot triumph in the light
overbearing me and pulling my heart
into the fertile decadence of pity.

I don't know what her song is.
I cannot hear her laughter.
Her flowers are in the hair
where I gracefully keep my longing eye.
She is something lost in the past,
a nimbus of mercy.
I don't reach far enough to her
to know where to place my truth.

Now when she smiles
the death definition expands,
and all chaos leaps unbounded
while I sit puzzled in the night.
I raise my glance to see her angel wings
dancing in the ashes.

Wait, the Phoenix of time
makes more mystery from illness
than love's own caresses.
I corrupt the emptiness with my longing.

I don't know her name.
I don't have it memorized.
Yet she calls to me in the holiday winds
and listens for the sighs in my heart.
Somehow I cannot bear this magic.
It cuts my passions and deals them fairly.

I am no longer worth having.
The soul is still.

I cannot object to the conscience

I cannot object to the conscience
I am presented with,
this nightcap caving in and loosening my eyes.

I gravitate to the yearning of all being.
Her name knows this, and she is only the truth.
No lie can exist in her heart,
and because of this I cannot have her.
I lie. I am a graceful icon.
My sharp arrows of fire
govern the sarcasm of her smile.

I know only what I am told to know.
I know nothing at all.
The last emptiness of my touch,
where I hide my mystic torch,
is the conqueror conjuring the brightness.

I pass a last moment to you
while you look into the mirror
heightened by your shiver...
the last thought cancels the edge
where I fall and singe my glance.

I am not surprised at your nod

I am not surprised at your nod.
You ask me to move forward
but like an angel in doubt
I hide my stolen fares.
Whisper in splendor,
I carry you in my old age
like a ring.
Fire is a majestic thing.
I cannot worry about you in faith
but I see you in the dark
wanting to be the light,
asking for a touch,
holding the bliss of symposium
in your cautious glass.

It's not the mirror that mocks.
Something in the soul bites.
Ice hits the wind and the scream
of hideous masks removed
makes the burns insoluble.

I open your letter for the last time.
The words have disappeared.
I don't know where you are.
I couldn't have lost you…
where are you?

Vulnerability cannot light the fathoms

Vulnerability cannot light the fathoms
of the sea.
If we drown, together we die
and the magic of song alights our thoughtful embrace.

I cannot write words, wise or unwise,
about where life takes us.
We are somehow in the same field,
tormented by the night
and waiting for stars to hit the final lockstep.
No one sees that angels don't exist for us.

I collapse. There are only four doors to our happiness.
No, we cannot predict which one will open quickest.
We cannot predict where our longings will go.
I see your man in the mirror,
his protective stare,
his hopeful eyes that wait for your return.
I can't hold you down when you have obligations.

Dark shiverings aren't counted by the clock—
I wait, I touch your face, my grace is exposed,
and my longing unhinged.

Love is a loss of words

Love is a loss of words,
waiting for black time
to return in the anxious splendor
of ancient envy.
I am perplexed by your sudden thrust
away,
but I know the moon is delight
and delight moves in sagacity always.

Your glow is deep like an abyss of fingers
touching one another,
holding the magic like dusky emptiness
as a threshold of fear.

Totality cannot take back
what it has given.
Nothingness strains behind hidden depths
like a rotten fruit fallen from the heights of our senses.

This is how worlds happen

This is how worlds happen,
the darkness mingles in the light
like two lovers who never resist each other.

They intertwine, hypnotizing
themselves into believing
there is a grander purpose to their mingling.
They never discover it
but their creations look at them
and reflect on their spontaneity.

One truth turns into another.
They lean on each other,
grieving and burning
like a small atom dying in friction,
becoming a grave of itself.
Nothing true dies.
Only we are alive.

As thinking beings,
we reflect the intensity
of night
as we succumb to the daylight.

If I was a serpent,
I too would tempt you
as only throbbing could.

The Greenest Dream

Once in the greenest dream - I seemed to have a friend,
but he left me in debt - to worlds I could forget.
His tone was like a string - vibrating on iron wings.
His verb I would not sing - as music in a dream.

When he left the globe - the promise I composed
was forgotten by him - whom I could not forgive.
The night crawled in my ear - leaving dread and cold fear,
and deeper will I clutch - memory as my crutch.

My mind cannot receive - the blessings of a dream.
His face is burned in me - like deadly poverty.
Condemn his ways to see - my own delightful beams.
Reluctance is not green. - It only seems to dream.

The Surrender

Fill the void of heart-sorrow,
let damask dreams slip into the darkness—
Freedom is the fearful touch nearby,
near the world's slanted eye.
How can I sing until tomorrow?

Net the fishes with cold bronze cups
and magic sighs.
Every force spins, like a spider,
upon the golden touch.

Fill the void, yes, with battles pure,
and the salt of seas
long forgotten.
Our wine cannot be tasted—
long have we wasted the surrender.

Jesus Shouting in the Elms

Sounds in the wind
bring fact and fiction together,
clearing one tablet of my life.

Hearts pulsate until the final quip,
and our usual selves pass reluctantly
into an inferior tower.

My cranium cracks and beholds
a sky of gold,
and Jesus shouting in the elms.

His skin dark and rough,
hair curled and oily,
and his eyes compassionately gazing.

I am frozen to the fixed beam
of his eye
He, brow knitted, moves closer.

"This pearl of wisdom, tiniest thing,
a fount of youth and peace.
Listen to its small quivering."

Stunned, I reflect on love,
and become the faithful image
that bears him along Golgotha.

Hill of shadow, skull place—
in my heart, empty, a promise is made.
The weak of heart are often strongest in love.

But the heart feels robbed, ungrateful,
its life seeking satisfaction in strangers.
I cannot see what I embraced.

I lose silver faces in the labyrinth
of my chest,
still searching, curious and silent.

❧

On the third day of the year,
we married our souls in union.
Then, as September passed into November
leaving only a shadow of our promise,
we console our hearts with thoughts
of eternal youth.

❧

Binding like child
to mother's dress,

separate though still clinging
to the lord of desire.

❧

Ovid

Burning face, offer me captured birds;
there is nothing in my eye like you.

I live for the night, cold and waiting:
there will be retribution around you.

Sweet music, tomorrow I shall hear:
I am deaf to a woman's touch.

But I must hear my heart in unique bliss:
I must stiffen under this hungry mask.

But I cannot live without your love:
I, too, am a lamp brisk and silent.

Wait

The river is full my love,
full of boasting desire,
waiting to be held.

The river is a dream
where words are parting
from succinct lips.

My desire is ripe
and overflowing with
affection.

I cannot fathom the depths
of the sea
I enter. I only know

how to wait.

Born from Old

A heart is one thousand sighs
and Death's chamber
is full of weeds.
That new flesh is born from old
is only a secret of time.

The Face

Then the face
comes
        closer—
what is it?

I am this *ghost*
of primrose
            heaven
where beacons
    are sweetly
    broken

swollen and
            startled
    by sad
        safety...
    what is it?
                the face
        in the door

    taller than death
        the night
                will break

Like War are Father and Son

This complaint must be heard,
but it isn't what I see
in that unholy light—
a dream without dreams.

No fight will kill the saint.
The truth is a mirror broken
across the moon's face.
The waters of time are channeled

over dirt and rags of space...
"Like war are father and son,"
say the beasts in the heart,
"we are sent to separate."

The purity of our lovely empire
that two-headed hydra of the heart
sets out to rip asunder!
But no beast is worth the worry.

Like war are father and son
and tide is without end,
but no one knows the tribal
will not last long.

Sapphire

The cold blue night
is still,
still as a blazing sun
in the dawn.
We move across the world
like nomads
in treasured rhythm.

Passion is a hazy thing,
a fog over weeping eyes.
Sapphire-colored wounds
open like structures
we do not know—
and my mind also whispers.

In the quiet and stiff silence,
a Buddha stares
like an ancient bird on a pedestal.
I cannot understand his eyes.

Mind is the substance by which
we divine light.
Suddenly, the thought escapes
from my troubled brain:
happiness is a choir
swiftly breathing songs as if they were air.

Bookstore Promises

The shadow of woman
faces me...
my heart expounds
like a worm spinning in the dirt.
I devour the concise fires
of oblivion,
the primrose circle of gargantuan Hell;
and spend money,
lavishing myself with hateful paradoxes,
mailboxes,
and the dreams of apes.

o Silence, how the children
know you,
believe you.
The faces of starling angels
in this perfunctory exercise,
arranged
like
bookstore promises.
The alphabet of rapture
is attuned by the ravages
of envy, the delightful little goat.

My mind's eye
is truly a river of fire
waving its insolent emptiness
around the cluttered aspect
where my icons burn

symbols are a reckoning
the yellow snake is my yearning
hiding in the faceless dizziness
of struggle and strife

the enemies grow nearer
and nearer to the compass
of day

&

I am as vague as a mumbling Christ
who tries to put the ties on the railroad
with only a crust of bread in his mouth

When the angels attend him,
he will remain solitary
like a prisoner confined in the doorway
where yawns signify Time

Open the coffers
where all the wisdom of the Earth
is crammed

think wide

January 1st, 1863
voice of Mr. Samuel Ealy Johnson, Sr.

I joined the Confederate cause
to fight the Union; only later did I believe
in problems with public solutions.
Progressivism was originally championed
by my Populist Party in Texas,
after the Civil War.

I did not suspect we would lose the war overall,
considering how desperately we fought in the Battle of
Galveston.
Two ships were sent from Houston to engage
the Union Fleet Commander, William B. Renshaw—
he put up a hell of a fight, setting off explosives
that killed his own men.

Accidents happen, I understand,
since I lost most everything to market forces.

January 1st, 1863 is a day I cannot forget,
even if I rest in this eternity of darkness.
I fought through the Civil War—
we recaptured Galveston Bay
and left the Twin Sisters as artifacts for our grandchildren.

My grandson, Lyndon B. Johnson, 36th President,
is rumored to have felt blessed because of me.
"I am lucky," he may have said, "to have a grandfather
who led such an interesting life."

The War Between the States was lost
for those siding with the Confederacy,
but I battened down my defeat
and continued to live until dying of pneumonia
at Stonewall, Texas in 1915.

Champion of Causes
voice of Mr. Samuel Ealy Johnson, Sr.

Time, they say, plays tricks.
I spent much of my youth fighting Union injustice,
and my grandson would
put away his teacher's chalk to fight poverty
through central governance.
The Great Society he called it,
and I know he knew that the root
of his progressive cause
began in Texas, with my failed Populist Party.

Democrats or Republicans, we were fractured as a society
and the parties were also torn by dispute.
We embraced direct election of Senators,
the eight-hour workday, currency issued by
the federal government,
and trust-busting, plus more:
all the causes we championed were taken up
by your modern liberals.
I spent my life like a gambler on adventure—
nothing I did amounted to greatness.
I lost the fortune I built herding cattle,
and depended on my brother for help.
We learned to pool our resources in troubled times.

I learned well that sometimes a man needs a hand,
and I was one man in a collection of many.
Oft forgotten I remain,
however prophetic my thought may have been.

My church *restrained* me from politics.
They thumbed their noses—
they booted me out.
I read voraciously
and could not care.
Happiness is a phantom thing.

Cuneiform

Clio governs me.
She reads my thoughts
like cuneiform,
and asks for amnesty
as she poses questions.

History does not lean on authority—
justice is determined
by superior principle and victory
in battle.
My mind is an ancient tablet
that contains the mysteries
of our human past.
Laughter lives like light,
and seeks the trust of darkness.

Clio is the numbness
in my soul,
that child's grief I sing to.
She sanctions the Mount
for dreaming too much.
Now we know beauty is a
matter decided by person
and conveyed through conquest.

Stubborn pipes continue to challenge
the cold winter night
while African tribes congregate
at the gate of daybreak.
The legend passed down
is our promised banquet:
loves and languished hearts
of surrender,
the minds of our ancestors.

I cannot skip my natural impulse—
I allow my body to convey
history,
to sink the cries of lost covenants,
to dream and dream under killing stars.

Sleepless

Harboring fugitives in the palace
of terror,
blank wrath will give me
the love i crave.

my heart, calling song or light:
i crave the existence
of peril, the
                    dark-
                    ness...

i will shrink the being
once I was
without seeking love
in quieter corridors:
deep, the listener will shriek
        of terror, a terror never heard.

i am awake yet sensing
nothing, sleepless as a silence
in the deep

Recordar

I am envisioning poetry.
My friend recounts a story
      about the knife he holds—
the Spanish word
meaning "A Memory"
is carved into it.

Yet, he ironically tells me,
the knife was given to me by my father
who has since *forgotten* the object—
      then he describes the pyramids carved into its handle.
You could scale a fish with this knife,
      the father prompted his son.

Taffeta

I hold you, softly,
and yet the guerrillas
will kill you
with silk.
Strangled, you radiate deeper
than the moon,
borrowing the cheerful chalice
filled
with my wine.

Sweet. I have taken the flight,
finally,
and talk to the seasons
like a dream conspiring with sleep.

Braced by the new evil and its skyscrapers:
i climb the heights
                    i sing the myth
                    to Thanatos.
Eros is still hiding in lullabies.

Lie in an Extra-Moral Sense

Truth and Lie
Walk hand in hand
To make report
Of the Land.
In my eye
Truth and Lie
Entertain a dark dream,
And in the alleys stand obscene.

Naked as birds in flight,
Truth and Lie speak of Right.
Is Right a step beyond
Truth or Lie's thick male bond?
Do these two usher consequence
Into life by inner sense?

Now what these two stars
Hold in their lights
Is an invitation to perilous night.
We all face the double bind
Of the bearded men, Truth and Lie.

Do Not Grieve

Meet toward the selfish center
of Time's complexities:
it must go on.
The sweet decadence of travel,
O Time, these histories are broken.

But we remain in the imagination's threshold.
No face is hedged in the wheel of destiny.
What is this piece of plain truth?
Ivory and ebony, o World, forsooth.
tTe music becomes mine, only.

Each language is a new trust.
I cannot hear the soft echoes,
silent in the distance.
O Mother, your times will not last.
Last though, o Truth, and do not grieve.

Liberty

Thereafter, the world contained sacredness
and sadness became unknown.
Thereafter, promises reigned superior in light.
I face the ignorant noise of society
and in privacy will become alert.
A monstrous noose hung above my head
like the sword of Damocles.

No demon and no soul–
the cause is dispossessed.
Without hankering forward, we find suicide
in the task before us.
Tantamount to treason, my speech uttered hypnotic.
Like redemption, the common man now rests
on the human throne.

Hercules Speaks to a Mere Mortal

In the dark, murder is like
a kaleidoscope,
turning inward and seeking life.

I break the legs of beasts
as if they were ancient fossils,
and think of life.

My heart pulsing and broken in two,
is my inspiration,
my own.

I cannot speak further
without questioning my words;
my motives are unclear.

Near the River and the Rain

That the Earth shall pass away
is sure,
but that an iota of speech remains
is uncertain.
Shall the particulars be unwed to the Muse?

The light will henceforth travel, free,
and the pastures of plenty
will be illumined.
Nothing, a bright emptiness of space and time,
will steadfast unite to the surrendering opus.

An oath grows near the river and the rain,
it is sweet.
Let wind travel at your feet.
The face will be unhinged–
and nothing will press forward therein.

desolation

desolation
                    pinches my heart
i feel lost and lonely
                        the invitation
but my resolution
                is to love
                without reservation
and know the barriers
                    are self-imposed

illucid dreams
                    lost to the houri
                    who have beamed down
                            like surreal clowns
                            undressing their white masks

Night Thought

The wind chatters loosely
and spirals through empty light–
Time's ladder I climb
healing as scars are carved
to weaken the past.

Each rung is a sense of death
and a certain risk.
Hope stings my heart suddenly
and turns a cold shoulder to my protests.

Bliss won't think twice before tearing
an opening in my thoughts.
I forget my hopelessness
as it decays in the night
    while I struggle to see.

Dory Williams is a 42 year old Texan who has been writing poetry for 24 years. She Loves movies and taking care of animals. Dory studied as an English major at the University of Texas at Austin. Recently she has been working toward health, independence, an enlightened view of Life and the poetry that reflects it. Publications include: Arthur Ford (in Pittsburgh), Iris Media Productions, Marymark Press (in New Jersey). Later publications include: Harbinger Asylum (in Texas), an online journal called "First Literature Review-East" and "Glimpse" by Alene Avason. Archived at: Yale University, University at Buffalo, and San Diego State University.

Dustin Pickering is a longtime Texas resident. He is the founder of Transcendent Zero Press whose mission statement includes "building creative community." He writes poetry, short stories, and is currently at work on a novel. He enjoys creating visual art and songwriting as well. He has long desired to begin an arts journal to promote freedom of expression, and successfully attained this goal beginning in 2010 with the publication *Harbinger Asylum.* He is the author of several poetry collections, some published in India. He also authored a work on aesthetics entitled *A Matter of Degrees.* He loves the oddballs, those who seek self fulfillment at all costs, and the ones who know the greatest successes are achieved through grit, failure, and reconstituting one's relationship with the world until the moment clicks.

www.ingramcontent.com/pod-product-compliance
Lightning Source LLC
LaVergne TN
LVHW011404080426
835511LV00005B/403